Fragrance in the Desert

Fragrance in the Desert

DEBBIE FOWLER

Fragrance in the Desert
Copyright © 2014 by Debbie Fowler
Second Edition

Book design by Jessika Hazelton

Printed in the United States of America

The Troy Book Makers • Troy, New York • thetroybookmakers.com

To order additional copies of this title,
contact your favorite local bookstore
or visit www.tbmbooks.com

ISBN: 978-1-61468-226-4

Acknowledgements

I would like to thank my dear, lifelong friends, Linda and Pam and my two extraordinary daughters Elizabeth and Amy Jo who listened patiently as I talked endlessly of my involvements overseas.
You supported me not just in word but in deed.

To my muses, Patty and Carolyn, thank you for your continual inspiration that has helped me know I was appointed to take on this task.

Special thanks and with much appreciation goes to my sister Cathy. Thank you for your countless hours of editing via phone calls, emails and even many road trips to my home. Without your enthusiasm, devotion and your belief in me, this could not have been completed. I couldn't have done this without you!

Last, but definitely not least I thank my husband John who has broadened my world, given me many opportunities of a lifetime and encouraged my passions through the years.

Dedication

To all those with no voice,

through no fault of their own,

that have suffered at the hands

of those involved in the crime

of human trafficking.

**I felt I have no freedom, I have no peace,
and it feels like I am in prison.
I wasn't happy, I cried every day,
I cried every single day.**

—Adjoua

*What I learned and
could not turn a blind eye to,
all started at a quilt meeting.*

Introduction

As a school girl, I was fairly quiet and shy. I know that may be difficult to believe for those that know me now. I was young when I first married, and placed in a role that required my attentions be given to many people. It stretched me as a person. But I grew in grace and learned what was needed, not only to fulfill my place as a young adult, wife and mother but in service to the church and the community. With much determination, I purposed to give from my heart to those I felt were in my care as a pastor's wife. I discovered I was a people person after all; especially to those in need of prayer, a meal, even a place to live for a season; and most of all a listening ear. I felt my role was to give and when you gave all you could, give some more. I didn't know back then how to be a pastor's wife, nor about being myself for that matter. Not knowing how to set boundaries, I played the role I thought was expected of me in this new life of mine.

Sensitive and compassionate by nature, I embraced others situations and needs as my own and felt their struggles and pain. In my desire to help, I negated the caring of my own inner needs. Through the years, "helping others" at whatever cost, cost me and my family. Little by little I became less and less until one day I broke and felt as though life was too difficult to manage. I was staring into a dark tunnel with very little light. I was diagnosed with clinical depression. It took some time to understand that living life day to day is really all about one's personal journey.

Early on, a friend encouraged me to "CHOOSE LIFE". It wasn't just to choose to live, but to choose to observe and embrace *life* itself. Choose to see it, hear it, breathe it, and feel it every day. Upon waking each day, I needed to choose life until it once again became as natural as my breathing. In search of the needed rope to climb out of the pit of darkness, and begin a journey of healing and hope, I began to explore art. Taking classes and the time at home expressing myself with paints and paper was a way to express and embrace life. While involved artistically, it gave me a break from the swirling thoughts that depression produced. I was getting stronger and there was a deep sense that pursuing creative art was feeding my soul, and giving me joy. I was experiencing life in a new way. As I continued on my journey, I came to understand that creativity could be demonstrated through every part of my life.

Being outdoors and appreciating all that has been created for our pleasure enhanced and furthered my grasp on life. Living in the North East of the United States offers the change of seasons year after year. I see them as a vehicle that steer me through life. Enjoying walks in a park, laughing as toads jump in ponds, feeding chickadees out of your hand, catching snowflakes with my tongue and, literally, taking the time to smell roses in the garden of life became essential and contributed to bring me new hope.

Changes occurred and I felt as though a new and stronger person was evolving. I felt adventurous and enthusiastic and my desire grew once again to know and share with others.

I remember praying in those dark days that what I experienced on this journey would not be in vain. My desire back then which still continues today is that I might share that there is always light and hope at the end of the tunnels in our lives. I couldn't have made it then and still can't today without the love and support of my family and friends.

Friends are angels
who lift us to our feet
when our wings
have trouble remembering how to fly
-author unknown

$\mathcal{S}ome$ events in life never get old or lose the thrill and excitement of the experience. Such was the case of the birth of our 9th grand baby. I had come in to town to be with the older children. While counting seconds between contractions with my oldest daughter, my husband, John phoned. He was very anxious to share his work day with me. (I was thinking *could you have picked a better time?*) But he couldn't help himself, and out he blurted "Want to take an overseas assignment?" He told me it would be for two years, with lots of opportunity to travel; three R&R's (rest and relaxation trips) per year plus two trips home.

This should have been a clue....
why so many R&Rs?

"Think of the places we could discover! Where have you always wanted to go Deb? We'll be able to save money for a house." I know he rehearsed his delivery before phoning me!

His enthusiasm excited me but it was also accompanied with skepticism. The adventurous soul in me was excited; the skepticism says this is too good to be true. Travel? A house? All of the possibilities were swirling in my head if we were to accept such an offer and then I realized I didn't know where! My mind wandered as he continued speaking. The ever romantic, I was visualizing the mountains in Austria, the Swiss Alps in Switzerland, maybe the streets of Paris or the Tuscany hills of Italy. "WHERE?" He echoes my question. "Uhh, Kuwait." And to my silence I hear him say, "You know, the Middle East". *Who goes to Kuwait? What kind of offer is that? Who accepts such an assignment?* This news gave me much to ponder as I waited for our little Gracie to arrive.

$\mathcal{S}oon$ after meeting my husband I was definitely smitten by what is referred to as the 'travel bug'. I have not been the same since. My husband, John, travels a lot for business and introduced me to adventures of a lifetime. It started out slow; I would accompany him for a few days, to places like Napa Valley and San Francisco in California. I went along to Austin, Texas and Kansas City, Missouri. One day, my destination dream came true. He phoned to say he needed to be in Scotland. Ever since I was a young girl, my heart's desire was to visit my home country of Scotland. I have never been as excited as when the plane landed in Glasgow. It was a dream come true. We treated each trip as if it were a once in a life time. We would say to one another; "we may never have this opportunity again." We purposed to explore the land, experience the culture, and see as much as we could in our allotted days. John would rent a car or we would hop a train choosing a direction, a turn here or turn there, chasing after mountains or castles we would see from a highway.

In our first year of marriage, a "once in a lifetime" trip to Zurich, Switzerland, happened three more times and we traveled all over Europe. Over the years, I traveled with him to the old cities in Spain, drove to the Mediterranean Sea in France, saw the ancient architecture in Greece, the Eiffel Tower in Paris, and traveled by train to the Swiss Alps. We rode through the countryside in Germany and up through the dolomites in Italy. Austria was one of our favorite places. It was not lost on us how often we felt "it was meant to be" to take a turn and find ourselves at an iron clad gate of a deserted castle, never getting tired of the adventure.

In more than one restaurant we found ourselves closing our eyes and just pointing at the menu because they weren't written in English and the waiter didn't speak it either. Meals were often a surprise. We ate foods we never heard of, met wonderful people along the way, learned to speak essential manners in several languages and understand the cultures and currencies. It was fascinating and exciting to have our passports stamped from all these different countries.

I remember the far away dreams I had as a school girl. So many lessons we had to learn, frequently had me wonder why it would be important to my life. Algebra class in 9th grade had me wondering that. And having to dissect worms in 7th grade was so disgusting to me that I walked out of class. But, sixth grade stands out the most to this very day. Mr. Johnson was my favorite teacher. He made learning fun. That year he introduced the countries of the world and we learned the customs of other nations. I remember pouring over the textbook filled with information and pictures and said more than once, "I need to go there! I want to see that!" Years went by, and life goes on. Traveling, and, experiencing different places wasn't planned for, nor a priority. But the seeds of desire to travel were planted in my soul at a young age.

I have traveled to places in the world I never thought would be possible. However, one of the areas I hadn't seen was the Middle East. Not that it was on my bucket list, but here I was, agreeing to take on another adventure.

I have learned over the years and am still a firm believer that everything happens for a reason. However, the reasons may not be apparent to us straight away. I also have learned that the path you follow in life is never a straight one. It can be filled with mysteries taking you through many life experiences.

Saying yes to Kuwait
was a journey
full of surprises.

The flight to Kuwait was approximately twelve hours. Those hours were filled with my fragmented thoughts; *it is an 8 hour time zone difference. It is a long flight. It's their morning when it's my night. Won't be heading back to America often…I don't know anyone…I'll meet people. The grandchildren will change so much, we'll talk on Skype….*and so the thoughts swirled. Very little sleep occurred on that flight. But, still it didn't deter my enthusiasm stirring up as the plane's landing gear engaged.

This is an adventure. It's for a few short years. I purposed to think of all the positives of this decision. I can do this! However, peering out the window to get a glimpse of my new home was sobering. I spoke aloud the words "OH MY GOSH, what have I agreed to?" These words crossed my mind more than once in the following two years. Scanning the horizon, I quickly searched for hills and mountains. There were none. There were no rivers and lakes. Even trees were scarce. What I saw was a sea of grit for as far as my eye could see.

Sand and lots of it.

The airport was crowded; it smelled of cigarette smoke and hot, sweaty bodies. Loud voices chattered in languages I had never heard before. Women in black robes and veils, men in white, some with turbans, all bustling through customs. Immigrant men with carts, ran to us; insisting they would help us with our baggage.

Out of the corner of my eye, in the midst of the bustle, I saw a group of young wide eyed girls being ordered to gather in a specified area. It was noticeable to me that they did not understand what was being said, and the order was barked angrily to them once again. Over the speaker in the airport, a loud monotone voice was heard, reciting prayers. I learn that there are designated rooms at public places for those wishing to kneel and pray. Six times a day prayers are heard at the airport, the mall, on the streets, in all the neighborhoods. There was no escaping that unfamiliar, haunting sound of prayers being broadcast throughout the day, *every* day, because Mosques were everywhere. Sometimes the prayers seemed sung over one another. Many small shops even close their doors for prayers.

The hotel's driver met us on the other side of customs. We were escorted through throngs of people weaving in all directions as well as whole families that were gathered to wait; grandparents, aunts and uncles and children of all ages. It seemed this was a place to be socializing as they waited for travelers; unlike America's airports where folks wait in the cell phone parking lot.

Crowds aren't something I enjoy too much; like festivals or even a visit to Wal-Mart. There are too many people, too much noise and confusion. So, to get past the crowds in the airport, I kept my eye on the exit door, anticipating the quiet and the relief to walk out those doors; only to find.... my breath taken from me. I couldn't "see" it, but it felt to me what I imagine fog would *feel* like. It was thick and heavy, the sense that I was trying to put one foot in front of the other in slow motion, while walking into an oven that I had just preheated to bake a cake. It was hot and suffocating.

The assault on my senses happened quickly upon arrival. Nowhere that we had traveled before prepared me for the culture shock I was just beginning to experience.

Kuwait is a Muslim country. Arabic is the country's language. Many Muslim women wear hijabs and burkas. There are many dark skinned people. I don't understand the religion or the language. I had read that 67% of the population of Kuwait is immigrants and that means there are many more languages I heard but didn't understand.

It didn't take long for me to realize there was much, much more ahead of me to experience in my next two years of living as an expatriate in this small country in the Middle East called Kuwait.

And so this journey had begun.

$\mathcal{O}ur$ furnished chalet was big and spacious. There were three bedrooms, one we used for an office and the other spare room was for my art. There were two baths, an open living and dining area and maid's quarters. *A maid's quarters??? What?*

(Most Kuwait homes have maids...and it was expected that we would too. Some expats did have, as the Kuwaitis do...maids, houseboys, gardeners, nannies and a driver.)

I initially laughed. *No way, that is absurd.* The idea felt so foreign to me. However, I thought to myself, is this one of those things when in Rome situations. Some new friends pointed out that by hiring domestic workers, we would be giving them a job, one for which they left their home country in order to provide for their families back home. I had put my foot down to hiring a live in housemaid to cook and clean. That was out of my comfort zone. However, our housing situation was a bit unique in that it was a "hotel" and that had cleaning staff and laundry service. I didn't want someone to come in every day, but eventually agreed to twice a week. They surely found me to be strange to turn down all this *help.* The one thing that I truly loved and was grateful for was that my laundry was picked up dirty in a little sac and delivered clean and pressed by the end of day, two times a week.

I was not accustomed to living in air conditioning *all* the time either. Even on the hottest days in New York, I would rarely use it. I love for a fresh breeze to sweep through my house, but found out all too quickly it was I who was sweeping ...dust and sand. Times of having windows open were very far and few between. There really was no such thing as breathing in fresh air. Sand storms were frequent and the very fine dust would seep through the cracks of the windows and under the doors.

We chose this place to live because of its location. It was necessary for John to drive into the city as well as drive the opposite direction to the work site. Basically, we lived in the middle of the desert. The "resort" consisted of a large hotel, a fine dining restaurant and vacation chalets that were set apart as a small neighborhood. All of this was behind patrolled security gates. It was secluded and unique for sure, and I felt safe. However, there were no local people living there, only others who were staying temporarily for business or Kuwaiti families on vacation. Most of my neighbors were employees who worked up at the plant. I was isolated in a resort in the middle of a desert.

The plan was to live in Kuwait as expats for two years. One of the biggest tasks was sorting out what we wanted shipped overseas, and put everything else into storage. The idea of living in a foreign country was exciting, however, there were a lot of unknowns that had a potential to be stressful.

I really had no expectations as to how I would spend my days but art supplies were certainly a priority for that shipment to Kuwait. As a later thought, I also included my sewing machine.

The other point of preparation was my researching all I could find about my new home. Before our move, I had made several attempts to contact a United States Women's group. The emails I sent bounced back, and phone numbers didn't work. I wanted to find these ladies! I figured, how difficult could it be hanging around there if I was with other American women. But there I was, in Kuwait, and still no American contacts. It took several weeks for our shipment to catch up with us. It was a very happy day when the pallet of belongings arrived!

The hotel staff faithfully provided daily newspapers to my front door. Reading the world news was particularly interesting from the Middle East point of view. I read about what was happening in Yemen, Iraq, Iran, Korea, Australia, US etc. It was definitely a more informative newspaper than my local paper back home.

I was now living in a foreign country on the other side of the world. I was more interested than ever on what was going on "in my back yard". (Seriously, the Iraq border was only forty miles away.)

The daily routine of reading the papers over coffee every morning, not only opened some social opportunities for me, it imparted more knowledge than I ever expected.

One morning soon after our arrival, I read a notice in the paper announcing a meeting of the Kuwait Textile Arts Association. It was to be held at the Sadu House that very evening!

It is very fortunate to live in a day and age that questions can be answered, with a click of a mouse. In my search I discovered the background of the Sadu House, and a website for the KTAA. With the help of a GPS, we made our way into the city.

The Sadu House is an artistic house and museum in Kuwait City. It was established in 1980 to protect the interests of the Bedouins and their ethnic handicrafts, Sadu weaving, which is an embroidery form in geometrical shapes hand woven by Bedouin people. The house originally existed as a mud building in the early twentieth century but was destroyed during the 1936 Kuwaiti floods. By 1984, Sadu House had registered 300 Bedouin women, producing about seventy items every week. A major tourist attraction in Kuwait City, Sadu House has several chambers each decorated with pottered motifs of houses, mosques etc.

SADU HOUSE

After the lecture, refreshments were served. Natasha greeted me with a warm smile. She was a most friendly woman from Russia living in Kuwait with her husband and family as an expat. She told me of the quilt group that was meeting the next morning and invited me to meet the Q8quilters.

My mom taught me to sew when I was a young girl. And as a teenager I made my own clothes and then in later years made outfits for my children. I even made a couple simple baby quilts when the grandbabies were born. I didn't consider myself a quilter; and certainly not the caliber of the women I eventually met. However, quilters were in my path and the America Women's Society was nowhere to be found. I decided I was going to learn to quilt. I became a member of KTAA as well as the Q8quilters.

I know now, that I had not connected with the American group because there was something more in store for me; an international group of women all living in Kuwait for the same reason; our husband's work. The stepping out to attend a quilt meeting as a non quilter has changed my life.

I didn't realize

at that time

all that was set in motion.

$\mathcal{W}e$ had one car between us. A shock to my independence! This was something new we had to work out. Being that the quilt meeting was the next morning, it became clear that I was the one hiring a taxi. Hire a taxi to go to a quilt meeting? This was a new experience in itself, and as anticipated, a bit on the scary side.

I had an address of a place I had never been, of a woman I had never met, for a meeting with strangers in a city and country I have lived in for one week. And I was alone with a driver from Pakistan who didn't speak English!

Round and round we went, in and out of neighborhoods. He stopped three times to show people on the street the address I gave to him as we traversed the city streets of Kuwait. Again those first thoughts I had as the plane landed just a week ago, "Oh gosh what have I got myself into?" were silently on my lips once again.

I did eventually get to the meeting. What awaited me was a whole new world. I felt at home as soon as I was seated. The room was filled with forty women who are passionate quilters, artists, and designers of fabric and paints from all over the world. Never have I been in a room of such a diverse group. I met women who became my friends from India, Malaysia, Canada and Germany, Venezuela, US, Italy, England and South Africa.

As introductions were made, I wanted to know, as did they, where are you from? Why are you here; and, how long till you go back? I giggled to myself on the way home that day thinking the questions about living in Kuwait sounded as if we were talking of a jail sentence.

Apparently, I was destined to be a quilter. I learned to appreciate quilting as an art and am now as in love with fabrics as I am with paints. Meetings were held twice a month in someone's home. Classes were offered by the more experienced quilters, and I enjoyed my days and weeks with these wonderful women. Bonds of friendship form quickly when living overseas as an expat. It is a transient community. Jobs are usually temporary so families come and go per assignments and/or they are traveling in and out of the country due to updating visas or taking those needed R & R's.

Driving defensively took on a whole new meaning in Kuwait.

It was always a stressful event to get in the car and drive anywhere. No matter whom the driver was. My heart always ended up in my throat.

Every day I saw dangerous and reckless driving and accidents right before my eyes; putting people's lives in danger and some even to their death. It was nothing to see four or five cars crashed and burned or rolled over along the roadside on a daily basis on the way in or out of the city.

Tailgating and lane weaving, most often at high speeds was normal; as was seeing children climbing over the seats. Apparently there were no car seat regulations here. I often saw children hanging out of windows or with heads out of sunroofs, and all too often, babies sitting on the driver's lap.

Even though, as a passenger I had experienced those unsafe driving conditions, I was still determined to establish some independence while living here in the desert. Driving in a foreign country has never intimidated me before. I felt confidant I could get myself to the city for groceries. Gosh, I do that every week at home. The trip in to town was uneventful. However, the return trip back to the chalet proved to be filled with quite a bit of drama, something that I had never experienced nor anticipated in all my years of driving. It seems that with the young men here, one way to get the attention of a female is to follow them; stalk them in your car.

I had noticed a car following me closely as I headed on the highway back to our home. It pulled up alongside me, and then fell back. This went on for a few miles and I was getting nervous. Then it seemed that he got lost in traffic, a sigh of relief from me until I saw him up ahead waiting for me to catch up and then pull right behind me again. This went on the entire 45 minute ride home. My knuckles were white, and I was shaking as I pulled up to the security gate that enclosed the chalets.

The security men in the booth knew me. We would always greet each other with a smile and a wave as they scanned the car and opened the gate. However, to their surprise, I jumped out yelling and pointing at the driver behind me (who had the audacity to follow me right up to the gate, by the way) the guards didn't understand. (Language barrier, no kidding) The young man stayed in his car with a smirk on his face and slowly backed out and went on his way. Is this a form of entertainment? Was he trying to scare me? Or, should I be flattered he thought I was some *young* female to flirt with.

The next time I needed to go out for groceries, I scheduled a driver from the hotel. Apparently there was a misunderstanding because he stood me up. I then learned he could not be available as a taxi service. I took a taxi the next week which was really not a pleasant experience. The filth and smell in the vehicle turned my stomach, as he dangerously drove the highway into the city. Aside from needing to grocery shop, I was meeting friends for lunch and attending meetings which meant traveling to the city several times a week. The cost of a taxi added up quickly. The only other viable option was to consider what was offered me from the beginning, to have my own driver.

Issues at week six

resolved!

His name

is

Haneef.

Anywhere I wanted to go, Haneef could get me there safe and sound. He would come for me on time, drop me off wherever I needed to be and returned for me any time of day or night. I enjoyed his company and we respected each other immensely.

My life became easier. No more worries riding into town with crazy taxi drivers. No more getting lost. No more cars stalking me. The first time Haneef took me out was to the grocery store. What a treat. As he pulled up in front of the store, he asked when he should return. When I got to the checkout line, I found him waiting. He greeted me and then proceeded to place my bags in the cart and take them out to the car. As I reached to grab a bag, he respectfully waved me away. At first it was embarrassing. The things I was accustomed to doing myself, were now being done by Haneef. Once back to the chalet, he would unlock the doors and bring in my packages as well. I have to admit, I got used to this kind of special treatment. It was great!

Haneef is a young man from Sri Lanka, who became not only my driver, but my guardian and friend. I felt safe. He knew where I was and where to find me. He was polite and respectful. He became a trusted friend. I no longer worried about the traffic, and antics on the roadway. Sometimes I would even nod off. My favorite part of each trip was watching out for camels. No matter which direction we were headed for the day, it was very rare not to see several camels along the way. Sometimes a whole caravan would either be grazing (not really sure on what) or just plodding along one behind the other. They really are the silliest looking creatures and they just make me laugh. Haneef was amused that upon each sighting I would exclaim and point them out to him as we drove down the highway. I suppose it is similar to pointing out deer when driving the thruway in New York; however, this is more common than the shy deer in our area at home. Sometimes I would see shepherds with their sheep along the roadways. They dress in white with their heads covered to protect them from the scorching sun; and they even carried a staff. It surprised me, that these scenes along the road are what I pictured the scenery of Bible stories so long ago.

Haneef would share stories and pictures of his family with me and I told him of my grandbabies in the United States. He was living and working in Kuwait as a domestic worker; his wife and young son were with family back home in Sri Lanka. He was saving money in hopes to bring them over to join him in this country. Imagine, servitude in Kuwait offered more for him and the future of his young family than what could be found in his homeland.

He began as a house boy, and then secured a job with a company that provides world businesses services in Kuwait. That is how we met him. My husband's company hired him to start as a driver for company business. (*And then I became his responsibility also*). He has, over time, expanded his job responsibilities and is an important asset to the company in Kuwait. This job enabled him to save the money needed to bring his family over and to also secure a future home for them to return to in Sri Lanka.

I felt honored the day he drove to our chalet and proudly introduced his wife and son to me. I think it somehow was declared somewhere that we are more than "business" related. They were a young couple with a little boy…in a foreign country…no family. I was a mom and grandma….in a foreign country with no family. We belonged together. Some afternoons he would bring them over to our home to visit and I would play games and read stories to his little boy.

$\mathcal{I}$ really looked forward to the quilt meetings. Twice a month we gathered. Any who cared to, brought a show and tell of a project they were working on or had completed. Most often someone would demonstrate a quilting technique and sewing tips were shared. There was also a lending library of quilt instruction books and patterns that could be signed out.

I observed through conversations at these meetings, that no matter what our cultural background, women have so much in common. We share basic needs and concerns no matter where we come from. We talk of recipes and crafts and have common hopes and dreams for our families. We worry about the future for our children and we share the basic need for friendship and belonging. And, so it seems, it is also universal that when a group of people gather there is

most always food involved. It was such a treat to taste each other's sweets from our country of origin.

At one of the meetings in August of 2010, one of the quilt members, Barbara, introduced us to her friend, Petra. Petra shared her involvement with a group that was helping other expatriate women. They were in need and we were asked for donations. The list was long. They needed everything; from clothing and food to household supplies, bedding, and even plastic grocery bags. Not much detail was shared except that it was for expatriates less fortunate than us.

At the next meeting, donations were abundant. Barbara asked the group if anyone was interested to volunteer their time to teach sewing and perhaps other skills. It was the *other skills* that I heard. I began to search my heart as to what I might offer.

My mind was swirling. As Haneef weaved through the streets of Kuwait to bring me home, I took the opportunity to ponder. I was coming home that day with so much more than just a new quilting tip.

The next day, I phoned Barbara.

We met for coffee and she explained her reasons for being so vague about the charity she was supporting. She told me involvement needed to be discreet, *for the safety of these women. It was even important that the location not be revealed.* I found this most intriguing. Who are these ones who need all supplies for living, and no one is to know about?

Kuwait is one of the highest income earning states in the world, how can this desperate need for the helpless exist?

DEBBIE FOWLER

$\mathcal{A_s}$ I would come to learn, the reality is that many workers are completely ignorant of the language, traditions, and culture of their destination land. Their goals are simple: to reach that foreign land, to work hard, and then to send money back home. Instead, their passports are seized, often right in the airport and they have no access to communication. They are employed as domestic workers, but are physically and mentally exploited. They often have to work more than 20 hours a day, are denied rest, and are forbidden to go outside or leave the premises unless accompanied by their "owners". To add to their sorrows, they are often sexually exploited by these employers. Their main task is to entertain with good food and sexual satisfaction. These girls and women have minimal negotiation power to refrain, and have no access to any sort of help. Quite often, runaway maids fleeing their tormentors seek refuge in their country's embassy, if they are lucky enough to ever make it there. Others seek help from trusted friends or maybe a religious group or church.

Alone in a foreign country, with no one to turn to, these women succumb to unspeakable treatment from their sponsors until the humiliation, fear, and pain exceed what little dignity they had left. They run from that broken promise of employment at the hands of wicked sponsors, and, as a last resort, they seek shelters, driven by fear of their sponsors' wrath.

During the time I was living in Kuwait, there was one government shelter. Others were unofficial shelters in the basements of embassies. At one point it was reported over 300 Philippine maids had been housed in the basement of the Philippine embassy. I wondered how many other embassies were also full of runaway maids. And then, how many domestic workers endured the abuse because their home country had no embassy to run to? How many saw that the only way out was to end their lives?

A lot of these girls were swept from the streets of their small villages and sold to sponsors. Sometimes a Kuwaiti who "buys" himself a maid from an agent may also have been tricked. He may have been told she is talented, can cook, speak the language only to find out she doesn't understand a word, or has never cooked a meal. The corruption is at all levels.

Recognizing the great need of some of these expatriates, the Salvation Army began a guest house to accommodate the helpless women in distress in July 2009. Petra worked behind the scenes developing networks of groups who would be willing to donate and invest time for these women in need.

A Kuwait Corps Officer of the Salvation Army wrote a letter for Barbara to share to help explain the situation and the need of the shelter.

The Salvation Army not only provides them with accommodation, but food and also the basic necessities! The number, though not constant, averages approximately 35-40. There is no fixed time for the government formalities to be completed and it depends from case to case. It could sometimes take even up to a year to have the paper work regularized for them to leave the country.

The Salvation Army works on several different aspects besides just providing them with shelter. One of the most important being the preparation and or equipping them to live better lives when they get back home! These young women came with nothing but the clothes on their backs.

Every day I learned, not just how Kuwait exploited domestic workers, but the whole Middle East and not just the Middle East but Asia too and not just Asia, but truly my own beloved country, the United States, exploited domestic workers. How can this be? I have lived a sheltered life. I don't believe our newspapers tell the truth of what is happening in the world around us. Or do they, and I have had blinders on....or minimized it in my mind....pushed it off because it doesn't affect me, therefore, it's not happening or its happening *way over there* on the other side of the world.

The days following that meeting left me shaken. I listened closely. I read carefully. I felt I had come upon something that was so horrific and heartrending, and it was right here where I was living. I thought this is a terrible place. How *can* this be?

With my eyes now opened, I read the newspapers differently, more carefully, and cut out articles that dealt with domestics and maids. I think I did so because I found myself in disbelief of the things reported. Somehow, the stack of newspaper clippings made it real and kept the passion alive in me.

> On September 14, a Nepali maid killed herself by hanging in her sponsor's house in al-Zahr.

> On September 15, al-Jarida daily reported about two suicide attempts by maids in Kuwait. Interestingly, the report went a little beyond describing the place and method of suicide, and actually bothered to look into the cause of one of the suicide attempts. The paper stated that an Indonesian maid attempted suicide in al-Dahar after being "mistreated and beaten up" by her employers, according to her complaints, and that her last resort to end the abuse was suicide.

> -On September 26, an Asian domestic worker attempted to kill herself by swallowing pesticide in her sponsor's house in the Sabah al-Nasser area. On the next day, a 40-year-old Indian maid attempted to end her life by overdosing on pills in her sponsor's house in Sulaibiya. She was taken to the Faranwiya hospital and had her stomach washed.

Migrant-rights.org exposed an alarming trend of suicides by migrant workers in Kuwait. Most of the suicides and suicide attempts are committed by domestic workers, the most vulnerable of migrant workers since they are excluded from the protection of Kuwait's labor laws, and because their work takes place in private residences.

> A 23 year old Ethiopian maid attempted to kill herself by overdosing on pills.

On Aug. 6 an Indonesian maid threatened to jump from the second floor after getting into a fight with her sponsor. Two days later an Asian domestic worker was found dead in a pool of blood in his sponsor's house after cutting himself with a blade.

August 13 a Sri-Lankan maid threatened to jump off a second floor of a building. Police were able to talk her out of it.

On August 18 it was reported that a 25 year old Sri-Lankan maid attempted suicide

On August 22 an Asian maid was hospitalized after attempting to jump

On August 25 a Nepalese hung himself

On August 30 a Pilipino slit her wrists on Sept….and on…..

(Attempting suicide is a crime in Kuwait; all the reports mention that the police opened a file against the victim. Yet there has never been a case in Kuwait where a sponsor was tried for driving his worker to suicide.

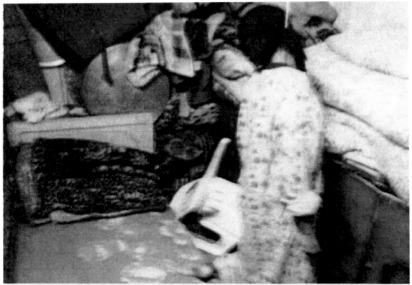

The body of the maid hanging from the rope tied to the ceiling.
Ethiopian Maid hangs herself to death

KUWAIT CITY, Jan 24: An Ethiopian housemaid committed suicide by hanging herself with a rope from the ceiling of her room inside the house of her sponsor in Taima.

Reportedly, when the Operations Room of Ministry of Interior received information about an Ethiopian housemaid hanging from the ceiling of her room in Taima, securitymen rushed to the location. They discovered that the housemaid had tied one end of the rope to the ceiling of her room and wrapped the other end around her neck

The corpse was referred to the Forensics Department. A Suicide case was registered and investigations are ongoing to determine the cause of the suicide.

By: Munaif Nayef Special to the Arab Times

$\mathcal{V}$ arrived at a very non-descript row of homes. The large wooden door opened after pressing a doorbell at the locked gate in front and we were greeted by Aban. She is an expatriate from India, living in Kuwait with her family for the last 20 years.

Aban quietly listened to our ideas, as we discussed with her how we could also be a support to the shelter. She is at the shelter every day. The Salvation Army hired her to oversee the girls welfare and the staff that work alongside her. She has much wisdom and insight and it is very apparent that her heart is with the women in her care, to see that they are safe, that they come to know God's love, with hopes as they begin to heal, they will learn that not all mankind is evil, deceptive and abusive.

During our visit there was no indication that currently there were twenty four women from Nepal and two from Ghana living in the house.

It was important for the girls to remain quiet. No one in and around the neighborhood was to know of their existence. They were not allowed to go outdoors for any reason. The sponsors they fled were most likely searching for them. Police would also be on the lookout and the risk of their being stopped was high. Not in possession of any identification papers, if stopped, they would be arrested and all attempts would be made to return them back to their "owners".

Does this not sound a lot like slavery?

There are three floors plus a full basement. We went down the stairs to an open room with chairs stacked to the side and a small alter. Six young girls huddled in their own thoughts of pain and grief...none speaking to the other. The atrocities they endured were personal. For some, Aban explained, the girls could not express in words. One dear one lay prostrate on the floor sobbing out her pain and begging for the memories of fear, and torture to be cleansed.

These sweet, vulnerable women had been raped, over worked, had little sleep and most were either poorly paid or not at all. Many of them had tolerated this treatment for months and years until it became unbearable. It is a desperate act to run. They are ashamed that they failed their families by running, giving up the opportunity to send money back home. It is a big risk to be on the streets without papers searching for help. They arrive at the shelter broken.

Now FREE from their captors they are still cursed and alone with their thoughts. They are learning to trust strangers once again, and seeking hope for inner peace. This room is their sanctuary. They can pray, sing, and cry with no fear of being heard and discovered.

The main level looked like anyone's home; with an open space of living and dining areas. A simple desk sat to one side where Aban could conduct her work. The small kitchen was barren. The next floor up had a small room used for sewing and another room housed a small television. On the third floor were just two bedrooms.

As I walked into one of the bedrooms, I found several girls sitting on the floor amongst a pile of plastic shopping bags tearing them into strips to be crocheted into pocketbooks, rugs, and bowls, expressing their own creativity to make designs in their "product" from the color printed on certain bags. They chattered softly as they worked, with the goal to produce enough to be sold at a bazaar, their only source of income.

It was very obvious these bedrooms had no beds. There were only mats and blankets folded in the corner of the room to be brought out at night. Not enough to go around, the girls shared what was there.

$\mathcal{W}e$ were introduced to three of the maids by reading their brief story they so bravely shared with the staff at the shelter.

My name is Rehka. I came to work in Kuwait as a maid through an agent who charged me 10,000 Ethiopian Birr. (Approximately $1,000 US) My madam did not like me very much. She would beat me up for little mistakes. They did not pay my salary for six months. One day she got very angry and pushed me out of third floor window. I fell on my head and was rushed to the hospital but madam lodged a case against me saying that I am crazy and jumped out myself. I was in coma for six months and when I regained conscious the hospital left me at the local Kuwaiti agency. I was a burden. I get dizzy spells, my legs and stomach hurts all the time and I cannot see with one eye.

My name is Maya. I am 50 years old. I am a widow and my two sons are married and have their own lives. I came to Kuwait to earn my living. My boss and madam were very nice to me. Last month when they went out of Kuwait for 10 days their two sons who are as old as my sons raped me repeatedly for two nights. All the time I cried and told them that they are like my children. When madam came back I told her what had happened. She got very angry and said I am ruining their reputation and sent me to the embassy. The embassy did not have place to keep me so I came to the shelter.

My name is Mary. I am a seamstress who was cheated by my agent in my home country and sent to Kuwait to work as a maid. One day I fell down the steps and hurt my feet badly. My madam accused me of being lazy and pretending to be hurt. She had not paid my salary for three months and when I asked her for it she verbally abused me. I ran away to a friend's place. My country does not have an embassy in Kuwait. It has been two years since I am without work or identification papers.

All who come to the shelter
have similar stories;
some, far worse.

Each in their own time, the girls began to trust and receive the compassion waiting for them, although, some never spoke of their horrors. They had been deceived and betrayed, they have no guarantee of freedom, for a future, and no guarantee of safety.

I understood the reason my husband needed to be in
Kuwait. And now I understood why I had come.

My ride home that day was with heaviness of heart. I was remembering the need for my own emotional healing many years ago. What I had "gone through" vs. what these young women have endured was not the same by far. However, there was this sense that what "worked" for me and was instrumental in my own journey of healing might bring peace and rightness into their lives. Perhaps, providing an opportunity to explore artistic freedom, they too would find strength within to continue.

I began planning artistic activities. However, in the back of my mind, I questioned my inclination to bring the art supplies the next week. Most of the women are very young and were in need of housekeeping skills. It was implied that to do some crafts would be fine to sell at a bazaar, but not something they would need to know once they were home. I felt naïve with my "hopes of healing" idea. How foolish I felt. Perhaps all that is important is learning life skills.

I was awakened to another reality that day and found it most distressing.

Thankful for the long ride home, I tried to sort out the emotions that were so upsetting.

How can these truths of humanity exist?

There were no supplies for the kitchen or the sewing room. We relied on donations for everything. The kitchen needed cooking utensils, pots and pans as well as ingredients for the pantry. We were in need of sewing machines, fabric and notions before we could think of teaching sewing. Little by little, support expanded for the safe house. Eventually, through other organizations, volunteers joined sharing something of themselves, teaching English, knitting or yoga.

Women were helping women.

Daily, supplies were dropped off to trusted volunteer's homes to be delivered to the shelter. Through Petra and Aban's efforts, other organizations gave donations of food, clothing, and supplies.

The volunteers brought calm to their spirits, a healing to their wounded and crushed ideal of humanity, demonstrating that good people do exist in the world. The house was bustling with kind hearted women day after day offering their love and support.

"We need someone to teach them cooking" is what Aban had said. Well, I can cook. So Thursdays became cooking class day. The two hour slot of cooking class always lasted much longer into the afternoon. A one morning a week visit quickly changed to two days a week. I seemed to always bring a carload of supplies from the quilters.

As weeks passed, a change occurred before our eyes upon entering the locked and gated home. Instead of the heaviness in the air of great sorrow and many tears, we heard singing, and giggles.

Some mornings when I arrived, I would be greeted by many of these precious ones lining up with folded hands to greet me saying "Namaste" along with big hugs when I entered the house.

The custom in Nepal when someone arrives, be it a store, home or office, any time of day, is to offer the visitor a cup of chiyaa (tea). They considered it to be incredibly rude to not offer a guest chiyaa. Likewise, it would be considered rude not to accept! Therefore, before any lesson began, there was a time to sit, relax and enjoy chiyaa with one another.

$\mathcal{M}ary$ is from Ghana. She is strong, motivated and an encourager to the other girls. She understands her talents, using them to teach others. She was very eager to learn, and instrumental in encouraging the girls in continuing on whatever sewing project we had begun. In the kitchen she was patient, helping me explain the recipes. As Mary translated, many of the girls wrote down the recipes and instructions in their native Nepalese, making their own little cookbooks.

The first week we made cutout cookies. It was quite something to do with twenty girls around the table. The oven was difficult to regulate. The normal 8-10 min baking time turned into 35-40 min. We learned that if we were to be baking, extra time was needed due to the slow oven.

Those were the best of days!

During one "waiting" time, thinking we may be better off learning something that doesn't involve the oven, I asked what they felt would be important to learn. Their suggestions surprised me. Their list included how to make pasta, yogurt, and cheese; all of which *I* have never made! Mary explained to me that the ingredients for these items would be available to them in their villages. As they waited for my response, I knew they were thinking *she hasn't a clue how to make any of this.* Mary then asked "Maam...you **can** teach us, **yes**?" We all began to laugh. I told them we will learn together! Once again, I was at my computer, this time learning how to make homemade pasta, yogurt and cheese.

Also during this waiting time I would bring out the totes of art supplies I had stored away in a cupboard; waiting for the right time. It was full of paper, glue, scissors and paints. Not one girl hesitated in choosing something from the tote. Exploring their imagination, they made cards; they sketched, and created designs. Some painted scenes of their memories of home. It was interesting to observe their choice of colors or themes. Sometimes they worked quietly and were reflective. At other times there would be much laughing and silliness.

There are no words to describe some things that burden the heart and cause us so much pain. However, given the opportunity and freedom to express artistically, I believe brought more than just a smile on their faces. They were eager to show their creations and desirous of acknowledgement and praise. As time went on, seeing the openness and excitement in creating, other volunteers brought ideas to make good use of our waiting time in the kitchen. Maryanne and her teenage daughter brought in polymer clay and taught the girls how to make beautiful pins. They were thrilled to learn a new craft. The designs and colors with the use of beads were all beautifully and uniquely made.

Another volunteer was a henna artist. She decorated hands, feet, arms and legs. And those who were interested were encouraged to broaden the use of their sense of design. Delighted, they took hold of the instrument and began to create on human canvas. These days were as I had hoped. Just plain fun! For a few short hours they weren't runaway maids. Their focus was directed away from the grimness of their current status. And they experienced joy.

We had a handful of regulars who enjoyed learning to sew. In a very short time, table mats and runners, quilts, pincushions and purses were completed. We would demonstrate a sewing project at our class and they took it from there. Working together they taught the others. We were always surprised and amazed at what was accomplished when we returned the following week. There were more smiles when we entered the house. And we could hear humming and singing as they tore plastic bags and crocheted slippery material

into beautiful bags and baskets. It was yet another outlet for creativity. They worked hard and were proud of the items they made to sell.

Aban and I represented the girls at two bazaars. The proceeds became their nest egg for their eventual return home.

Sometimes those long wait times for whatever was baking became language lessons. They enjoyed teaching me their native language with much laughter at my mispronunciation and forgetfulness and would giggle unmercifully at my attempts! I would take notes and practice at home because I knew they would test me the next week. I was failing miserably. We shared many laughs in that kitchen. They would pick up bowls, a spoon, flour, sugar....making me repeat after them. We resorted to pantomime in order for me to understand. Over and over we acted out my coming into a room saying hello, I'm here....how are you...please sit down... would you like tea? One day they put their hand to their ears pretending to phone me. They asked for my number so I gave it to them, even though none of them had a working phone. And they continued to practice making a call.

"Hello Ma'am....we are in Nepal...we Love you"

We all laughed and hoped for that day.

**I was no longer seeing sad,
forlorn faces,
but
the sweetness
of new hope and life.**

Their status hadn't changed. No one knew when or who would have the opportunity to return to their homeland. With so much red tape in a dishonest society, it takes a long, long time. In the meantime, they lived each day learning new things about themselves through the creative process in sewing, cooking, painting, and singing. They were choosing to live each day. Their voices soared and their eyes began to sparkle.

My days at the shelter brought meaning to me in Kuwait. Tuesdays and Thursdays were the best days of my week. Some days I was just a person who stopped in like she said she would; no cooking or sewing completed but lots of hugs, art and language lessons.

I had been awakened to another reality of life in the Middle East. Many days we drove home in silence and I would wonder how Haneef felt about my involvement with the shelter. We didn't speak of it, but I knew he was aware of what I was doing at this seemingly quiet house that I visited every week. Some days I had many bags and boxes. Being the ever gentleman that he was, he would unload the car and want to bring the items inside for me. I was nervous about this, not wanting to put him in any compromising position.

One day with his warm and infectious smile, as I gathered up supplies, he picked up my bags, gazed up to the house where the maids were "hidden" and back at me with the look of understanding as to *what I was up to*. We just nodded to one another as he said with a smile, "Ma'am, its okay I am here for you". From then on he assisted me in to the shelter. He chose to support my efforts. (He also became the recipient of our cooking and baking.) He was always waiting patiently at the end of the day to drive me safely home.

I was raised to respect all human beings and taught about civil rights regarding equality, and my belief is that we are all created equal.

> The concept of diversity encompasses acceptance and respect. It means understanding that each individual is unique, and recognizing our individual differences. These can be along the dimensions of race, ethnicity, gender, sexual orientation, socio-economic status, age, physical abilities, religious beliefs, political beliefs, or other ideologies. It is about understanding each other and moving beyond simple tolerance to embracing and celebrating the rich dimensions of diversity contained within each individual.

On one occasion, an attitude of a volunteer surfaced. She too, was an expat now living in Kuwait for several years. As we prepared and waited for the girls to arrive in that humble little kitchen she shared with me her experience employing maids. Her opinion was that "they are simple." She likened it to raising teenage daughters. You must be stern with them; they are in need of discipline not love. She believes that the maids are "50/50". Some work out, but the rest are bad girls; home wreckers and thieves.

I had offered her a ride home that afternoon, (which meant I was really asking Haneef to drive her home). As she gave him directions, I noticed a change in her voice, as well as her body language. It was one of demand and an attitude expecting how she should be treated. Her attitude and voice changed with *MY* driver! Attitude, arising once again, that she was better than he.

I have seen this demonstration of superiority with immigrants in general; in the marketplace, restaurants, and playgrounds. Most were dressed in blue following behind those dressed in black. Often I would hear sharp commands directed to the maids. Even the children spoke with a disdain and disrespectful tone. I observed more than once when eating at a restaurant, how it was not uncommon to see the maid caring and feeding the children, while the parents ate their meal, either at another table or just at one end. There was no place setting for the maid. Superiority and arrogance was evident between the employers to the employee. Prejudice is blatant.

It seemed as though everywhere I went, the concepts of equality remained in my thoughts and weighed heavy in my heart as I acclimated to my new surroundings. My thinking and understanding was being challenged every day. I was observing servitude, slavery.

I discovered the following article written by Amanda Kloer on Change.org

In Kuwait, Domestic Workers Are Exploited and Unprotected

With almost 660,000 migrant domestic workers in the country, Kuwait has the highest domestic workers to citizens' ratio in the Middle East. And according to a recent report by Human Rights Watch, many of those workers face abuse, exploitation, and slavery. Sadly, while exploitation of domestic workers may be rampant in Kuwait, it is not unique to the country.

Latha traveled to Kuwait from Sri Lanka to take a job as a domestic worker. When she arrived, however, the job was far from what she expected. Latha was constantly watched by her employer. She was followed all the time, even on trips to take the garbage out. She was also beaten on a regular basis and locked indoors to prevent her from leaving. One day while being held in a locked room, Latha decided enough was enough. She fashioned a rope from bed sheets and climbed out the second floor window. While Latha survived her dangerous escape method, other domestic workers have fallen from windows or otherwise injured themselves while trying to escape slavery and abuse.

Despite the huge population of migrants like Latha who work as domestics in Kuwait, and despite the many well-documented cases of serious abuse and human trafficking which have occurred there, Kuwaiti laws do not protect migrant domestic workers from abusive employers. When domestic workers try and escape like Latha, the law allows their employers to charge them with "absconding" and have them deported. When workers are injured trying to leave abusive households, police often deem the incidents "attempted suicides." And if employers are wealthy and well-connected enough, they can get away with just about anything.

In addition to the complaints of forced labor or human trafficking, domestic workers in Kuwait have cited nonpayment of wages, physical abuse, sexual harassment and assault, and a refusal to grant days off or pay overtime. But domestic workers' exclusion from even the most basic protection labor laws provide makes it incredibly difficult for a worker to bring a case against an employer. Add that to the fact that many workers have families relying on their wages back home and the fact that some migrants may be undocumented, you've got a giant, desert-filled petri dish for human trafficking.

> Sadly, the exploitation of domestic workers and their exemption from legal protection is not unique to Kuwait. It happens around the world, including in the U.S. In America, domestic workers are left out of legal protections just like in Kuwait, and like in Kuwait, that means they have few avenues to seek assistance. But that can change if all 50 states follow the example of New York, and pass a Domestic Workers Bill of Rights, which would entitle domestic workers to legal protections. Please, ask your state legislature to pass the critical legislation today.
>
> Amanda Kloer is a Change.org Editor and has been a full-time abolitionist in several capacities for seven years. Follow her on Twitter @endhumantraffic

Did I just read that last paragraph correctly?
This happens around the world?
In the United States?
Oh my gosh!
Where have I been?

$\mathcal{W}e$ definitely experienced culture shock. Some days more than others it was a strain and stress to live in the Middle East. Although there are many stores and restaurants familiar to us in America, it gave the sense of "just like home" but not quite. Leaving the mall one evening we ended up in a traffic jam. Right before us on the busy city streets, a farmer was ushering a herd of sheep to take to market for the next day. It's just something you wouldn't see in a busy city in the United States. Some days the heat would be totally suffocating. Walking from the chalet to the car, I could feel my necklace begin to burn my skin. Sand storms would arise without notice and sometimes it was necessary to wear face masks. Rudeness in the marketplace, toward other expats was common as was rudeness on the street. I found myself diligently searching the streets, the stores, even checking out people in their cars, looking for a *western person*. Mostly my observation was of people very unlike myself.

We never felt afraid although there were occasions that I suppose we could have been. The Middle East countries had uprisings to their governments all around us. There were demonstrations in Kuwait City that the US Embassy sent warnings to us via email. One afternoon I heard in the distance shouting and sirens, from our backyard; demonstrations were happening only a mile away. *It became clear why the company awarded the R&R's*

My morning routine of reading the Arab Times continually educated me about the world in which I was living. There is no perfect country, city, or neighborhood anywhere in the world. Certainly one can choose to focus on one specific topic or theme when they read a newspaper. However, I found a "theme" that demanded my attention.

I began to clip out my findings.

I wondered as I read, were these accounts similar to what "my girls" experienced? What unspeakable acts were still tormenting them?

Sri Lankan maid alleges nail torture in Kuwait

HRW issues Kuwait report

Abuse of maids seen rising

KUWAIT CITY, Oct 6, (Agencies): Abuse of domestic workers in Kuwait is rising, and maids in the country face prosecution when they try to escape, Human Rights Watch said on Wednesday.

The New York-based rights group said migrant domestic workers have minimal protection from employers who withhold salaries, force them to work long hours with no days off, deprive them of adequate food or abuse them physically or sexually.

"The number of abuses has been rising," Priyanka Motaparthy, HRW research fellow in Middle East and North Africa, told a press conference announcing a report, which details specific cases.

"In 2009, domestic workers from Sri Lanka, Indonesia, the Philippines and Ethiopia filed over 10,000 complaints of abuse with their embassies," she said.

The HRW data does not include Indian maids, who represent almost half of the 660,000 domestic workers in the country. Domestic workers, almost entirely Asian, form one-third of the 1.81 million foreign employees in Kuwait.

The 97-page report, "Walls at Every Turn: Exploitation of Migrant Domestic Workers Through Kuwait's Sponsorship System," describes how workers become trapped in exploitative or abusive employment.

"Employers hold all the cards in Kuwait," said Sarah Leah Whitson, Middle East director at HRW.

The report was based on interviews of dozens of runaway maids at either their embassies or a small government-run shelter.

Domestic workers in Kuwait are not covered by any law to limit working hours or a rest day or even basic rights, the report said.

"They are forced to work for unlimited hours, 10, 12 or 18 hours with no breaks, seven days a week, 52 weeks a year," Motaparthy said.

Manik J., a Sri Lankan, said she had worked for more than 18 hours a day for 10 months, but did not receive her salary for most of the period although she worked for two families. She was at the government shelter.

Twenty-one domestic workers interviewed by HRW said they had worked 18 hours or more per day on repeated occasions. A 2004 International Labour Organisation study found that maids in Kuwait worked for 101 hours weekly, HRW said.

The main abuses include physical and sexual abuse, non-payment or delay in payment of salary, long working hours, no weekly rest day and others, the report said.

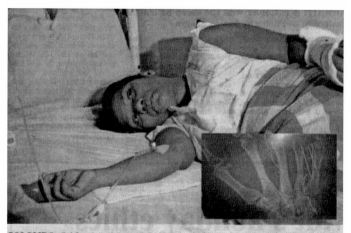

COLOMBO: Sri Lankan housemaid V R Lechchami, 38, lies on her hospital bed in the northwestern town of Kurunegala yesterday. (Inset) An X-ray image shows some of the 14 steel nails driven into the hands of the maid. — AFP

Sponsor 'hammers' 14 nails into maid's body

Sri Lankan alleges nail torture in Kuwait

COLOMBO: A Sri Lankan housemaid has accused her Kuwaiti employer of hammering 14 nails into her body, in the second such incident in the past few months, a local doctor said yesterday. The woman, identified only as Lechchami, 38, underwent surgery to have the nails removed after returning home to Sri Lanka, the director of the hospital in the northwestern town of Kurunegala said. "We have removed nine out of the 14 wire nails that showed up in X-rays," hospital director Soma Rajamanthri said.

The doctor said the woman had told surgeons that her nails into her hands and left leg — some as long as 3.5 centimeters — when she asked for her salary after working for six months.

Continued on Page 14

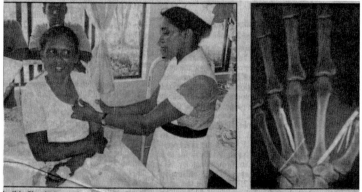

In this file photograph taken on Aug 25, 2010, Sri Lankan house maid L.T. Ariyawathie (left), who returned from Saudi Arabia with 24 nails inside her body, talks to a nurse while receiving treatment at a hospital in Batticoloa. (Right): This file photograph shows the detail of an X-ray film held up by a doctor of nails driven into the hand of Ariyawathie. (AFP)

Sponsor 'hammers' 14 nails into maid's body

Continued from Page 1

"We can't verify her story, but she said the husband-and-wife couple who employed her did this to her," Rajamanthri said. A police spokesman said the case was under investigation. In August, another housemaid complained her Saudi employer drove 24 nails into her arms, legs and forehead as punishment. Most of them were removed by surgeons at Sri Lanka's Kamburupitiya hospital.

The Saudi government and private sector officials in Riyadh have questioned the credibility of the woman's allegations. Some 1.8 million Sri Lankans are employed abroad, of whom 70 percent are women. Most work as housemaids in the Middle East while smaller numbers work in Singapore and Hong Kong, seeking higher salaries than they would get at home. Non-governmental organizations report frequent cases of employer abuse of maids who work abroad. — AFP

Nails pierce world of Asia's migrant maids

COLOMBO, Sept 16, (AFP): L. T. Ariyawathie said she got a taste of what was in store for her just weeks after leaving her native Sri Lanka to work as a housemaid in Saudi Arabia.

At first, she said, her employers mocked the basic Arabic she had learnt during a 15-day training course before she left for the Gulf. Then, events took a more sinister turn.

"The torture started when a plate was broken by accident. (My employer) asked me whether I was blind and tried to prick something in my right eye," the 49-year-old said.

"When I covered it with my hand, they pricked a needle on my forehead above the eye."

Ariyawathie returned home from Riyadh last month traumatised after what she said was months of beatings

Continued on Page 8

Nails pierce

Continued from Page 1

and abuse. Doctors had to operate to remove dozens of nails and needles driven into her forehead, legs and arms.

Maid forced to 'swallow' nails

COLOMBO: Sri Lanka is probing allegations that one of its nationals employed in Jordan was forced to swallow nails, in the third case involving alleged torture in three months, an official said yesterday.

Continued on Page 14

Maid forced to 'swallow' nails

Continued from Page 1

A housemaid identified as D. M Chandima has told the Sri Lankan diplomatic mission in Amman that her employer forced her to swallow six nails, an official at the Foreign Employment Bureau of Sri Lanka said. "We are awaiting a full report from doctors," the head of the bureau, Kingsley Ranawaka, said adding that the authorities would decide on the next steps after looking at the medical evidence.

The report came as another Sri Lankan housemaid who had been working in Kuwait accused her employer of driving 14 wire nails into her body as punishment for failing in her work. The woman, identified only as Lechchami, 38, underwent surgery to have the nails removed after returning home to Sri Lanka, the director of the hospital in the northwestern town of Kurunegala said on Saturday.

The doctor said the woman had told surgeons that her Kuwaiti employers drove the nails into her hands and left leg-some as long as 3.5 centimeters - when she asked for her salary after working for six months. Police said the case was under investigation. In August, another housemaid complained her Saudi employer drove 24 nails into her arms, legs and forehead as punishment. Most of them were removed by surgeons in Sri Lanka.

The Saudi government and private sector officials in Riyadh have questioned the credibility of the woman's allegations. Some 1.8 million Sri Lankans are employed abroad, of whom 70 percent are women. Most work as housemaids in the Middle East while smaller numbers work in Singapore and Hong Kong, seeking higher salaries than they would get at home. Non-governmental organizations report frequent cases of employer abuse of maids who work abroad. — AFP

During this time the Human Rights Watch wrote their report on DOMESTIC ABUSE in Kuwait...each day as I read the articles a fire was burning deep in my soul and I was motivated, and determined to make a difference.

> Abuse of maids seen rising....and maids in the country face prosecution when they try to escape. (Human Rights Watch) in 2009 domestic workers from Sri Lanka, Indonesia the Philippines and Ethiopia filed over 10,000 complaints of abuse with their embassies. "Employers hold all the cards in Kuwait" said Sarah Leah Whitson, Middle East director at HRW.

I spent many of my days researching organizations that exist and other ways to help those that we volunteers fondly referred to as "our girls".

My heart became angry with a people, a nation, whom I was already not very fond of. In America we have avenues to make our opinions known if unhappy, or want to see change in what is occurring in our nation. Carefully I drafted a letter to the American Ambassador to Kuwait, having it hand delivered.

I wrote a blog for my friends and family to share my experiences of living in Kuwait and of our travels. But this part of my life overseas, I kept private. I shared with a few of my closest and trusted people. They listened to me and heard the burden of my heart.

My close friend and her husband shared my stories with their small congregation in Northern New York. The church has a Christmas tradition in that they select a group to bless financially by having a special offering. These folks gave so generously. They didn't know me. They didn't know these women. Not many people would have any reason to think or care about maids in a little country on the other side of the world.

Except
a caring
God

The gift was $8,000.

When I was handed the check, I humbly stood there with tears streaming down my face. My heart choked my voice as I realized the orchestration that took place in the hearts of so many people for this particular need. I was taken aback that I was trusted to be the eyes and ears, even the heart to share the realities I discovered in this foreign land.

Do these people know how great a gift they gave? Do they understand how far reaching this went to people they don't know, and would never meet?

I was privileged to deliver the gift to the Salvation Army and experience the gratefulness and tears of appreciation.

My daughters also heard my heart and they too joined me from across the world to show their support and *do* something. Amy Jo hosted a Christmas gathering of her friends and shared my discovery. Donations were brought together and they made kits of sewing and craft supplies. My sister and niece joined in cutting squares of fabric and boxing things up. These supplies were very much needed for the girls to continue creating craft items to be sold at bazaars, earning a bit of income that when the day came, they would indeed have something to bring home. Meanwhile in Wisconsin, Liz and her friends were packaging small gifts of personal items, such as nail polish, new socks, and earrings. They were beautifully wrapped in Christmas paper for each of the girls.

What does this say to me? There are issues in this world, heartache and need. One voice in Kuwait speaking passionately brought people together to make a difference. Upon hearing that voice, hearts were burdened with "what can I do?" And together, we did make a difference at that time. One I hope none of us will ever forget.

> **"One person cannot save the world**
> **and solve all of its problems**
> **but many people living in service to their highest calling**
> **will collectively lift the world**
> **and create light**
> **where it is most needed."**
>
> – Christine Mason Miller

One Saturday, I received a call from Aban that shook me to my core. Without notice, eleven girls were picked up and taken to deportation to be sent home. I was happy for my girls! They were going home! But, I cried terribly. Not only had I missed the opportunity to say goodbye, but I felt that I failed them by not being there. I hadn't been able to give them the special packets I had been preparing in secret for months. Now they were gone and my heart was very sad. I didn't want it to just end without being able to provide these girls with more, beyond a place of refuge and healing and a bit of cooking and sewing lessons. Do we just say our goodbyes and watch as they head back to the same place, amongst the wolves from where they had come? There had to be some-where to send them back to, a place that would help them continue on their road of healing and to live a better life.

The airline will get them back to Nepal but then what? Where do they go? How will they pay for transportation home? How will they pay for a meal? And what if they are not wel-comed home; where will they go? How will they eat? Where will they live? Will they face a desperate life once again and be lured back into a life of servitude and false promises?

A few weeks prior to this, I had begun research; looking for organizations that aided those that had been exploited. My goal was to provide each girl a packet with information to find a place where their healing could be continued and they would be supported in the reentry back in their home country and village.

With appropriate fear for the women I had come to love, I was motivated beyond giving out hugs and making pasta. My days began and ended researching, writing letters, making phone calls and learning all I could about human trafficking.

I learned of organizations all over the world that offered such support. Serious internet research was taking place in the desert chalet. I was driven with passion. Some days I felt I couldn't write fast enough; or call someone quick enough to share the ideas and information I had discovered.

> **"Whatever you think you can do, begin it.**
> **Action has magic,**
> **grace and power in it".**
>
> - Goethe

When I arrived at the house, the mood was bittersweet; such a mix of emotions. We all were happy for those who were called, but understandably sadness overcame the ones who remained; wondering when or if their time would come. No sewing or cooking took place that day, just a lot of hugs and support.

Aban, Barbara and I talked of the sadness we felt and how we were robbed of the opportunity to say goodbye. However, I thought, today they are home! But that point of optimism was met with Aban revealing that it wasn't the case. They were still in Kuwait, sitting in a deportation hall waiting and it could be a couple days or weeks before they fly home. My mouth opened, but no audible words came out. I thought, once again…*OH MY GOSH how can this be?* Now I understood even more the reason for such mixed emotions when authorities arrived. Some were happy to be going home. And some were fearful of families who would be disappointed that they hadn't met financial expectations. Fear of the unknown as to their treatment and safety, fearful of police, would they be fed and cared for or could they be once again abused as they wait for deportation.

Tears were shed
because we would miss our
"didis"
(sisters).

The days that followed were somber; the girls were continually on my mind and we all wondered if it would ever be known what became of them. My heart was sad and worried.

It was the ninth day since they were picked up from the shelter when I received a call. Immediately I heard many excited and sweet voices talking all at once in a language I have heard before. *Could this be possible?* The phone was passed around and I heard all of them trying their best to make me understand.

Ma'am, ma'am
we
are in Nepal!!!

Knowing they understood English better then speaking, I started asking questions. Are you my girls? Are you in Nepal? Are you safe? I heard giggling and many "yes ma'am...we are here, we are safe" and we spent the next few minutes giggling and shouting to one another "I love you, I love you."

I was sorrowful that I didn't have the packets of information complete and ready for these girls as they were now embarking on another chapter of their journey. However, I take comfort and am thankful for what had been shared.

Love,
trust and a
Kuwaiti phone number

These dear ones called with hope and encouragement in their voices. I will never forget the influence that few minute phone call continues to have on my life. They motivated me to search out, speak out, and to keep doing something on behalf of "my girls".

Another six months passed. I was preparing for my return home to America. Saying goodbye was heart wrenching. I had planned my last day at the shelter to be one week before my flight...so as to have time for packing and other goodbyes to my quilting friends. However, Aban phoned requesting me to come back one more time. Oh goodness, it was so difficult the first time, but I couldn't stay away. The girls had planned a farewell party, complete with a meal they cooked themselves! I spent the day before my departure, with "my girls". Not only did they prepare a meal but also a time of reflection and thankfulness of our time together. As we sat in a circle in the basement sanctuary, they sang songs of thanksgiving and love to God, and overwhelmed me with their gratitude. Each one took a turn to speak having Aban interpret for them. It was most humbling. Many tears of love were shed and heartfelt hugs given.

With tears streaming down my face I humbly stood before them. My voice found words to express to them how they changed my life. At that moment, I promised and declared I would never forget them and what they taught me. I promised to work hard and proclaim the truths I had learned about the ugly reality of human trafficking, and to encourage others to open their eyes to see and their ears to hear and their own hearts to take action.

I have been embarrassed of my ignorance. It took living in the sand to pull my head out of it and act. I can't turn a blind eye any longer. I spent time with victims of this horrendous crime...***this is real***. My hope is that my experience in the desert has stirred up a truth that you too won't be able to turn from; that you will find your way to make a difference also.

This wasn't just a visit to another foreign country. By living in the Middle East, I was introduced to a reality that affects the entire world.

**In the midst of the horrors I discovered
the sweetness of innocents
who provided fragrance in the desert.
My eyes have been opened
and I am changed forever.
I learned of the runaway maids.**

$\mathcal{T}wo$ years have passed since living in Kuwait. All the maids that were at the shelter when I was there have been extricated to their home country; all but one.

With the availability of social media, she and I have connected. I asked if she would be willing to share her story.

Her name is Adjou; a young woman from Ghana. I met her at the shelter in 2011. She is currently working in Kuwait for an American family as a nanny of three children as well as their housemaid.

She has an old laptop and can receive emails and is even on face book. That is how we found each other again. I had written to her, telling her I wanted to honor my vow to do what I can to expose the truths I came to understand. When I asked her if she would help me by answering some questions...she wrote back *"I am ever ready to answer all your questions and you can use my first name if you want to"* At her suggestion we met up on Skype. With a few promptings from me, Adjou told me her story.

I arrived in Kuwait March 6, 2009. At home in Ghana I worked as a cook. Through a friend I heard of a company in Kuwait that was looking for teachers and caterers. We never heard of Kuwait before....but learned it was an Arabic country. Dad went with me and paid $500 KD. (approximately $1800.00)

When we got to the airport, two men met us. They were from Nepal and Jordan. When we met them, they told us we would be doing housemaid work. We said if that be the case, we want to go back home. We cried and cried. We wanted to go back home. We cried a lot. And decided if the money we paid for this opportunity is gone, it's ok! We care about our lives. They should let us go back home. They said no. They said we had to work in a house. Then, after three months working as a housemaid, they will find me a job to work in hotel. So, again, we said "NO. You already lied to us in Ghana." So what else can we believe? But they took us to Kuwait houses. We couldn't do anything about it.

It was a shock when they told us. This wasn't what they told us in Ghana. We don't do that.....we are like family we try to help others to achieve something, to learn a trade, like sewing or hair dressing. That's the kind of people who go to do housework, for their families, not strangers. For me, I already completed my schooling and I was working. So bringing me to work as a maid, that was like no! This was no better. (Than in Ghana)

I wasn't happy. I cried every day. I cried every single day. The woman I worked for never saw me cry but she knew I was not happy. After working for one month I say to her, "no. I can't stay in this country, I have to go home." She took me back to the agency, but they just sent me to another house. I was cooking and cleaning, washing and ironing...it's a lot of work. Like I said, we don't do that in Ghana...we don't do that.

Were you mistreated?

Yea, of course. The way they talk to you....the one I was working for, she took me to her mother. A lot of housemaids were there...we were all working and I was crying...... I sat down for some minutes and the mother came to me and slapped me, she say ...why are you sitting? I can't have rest. Work, work, work...till it's time to sleep....one or two o'clock in the morning.

So even the women were harsh?

Oh Yea. The women mistreat people and the men mistreat people. Honestly, there are good people among them and there are, worse people among them.

After two months, the agency took me to another house.

I worked there for eight months. The eighth month is when my father died. This is not getting any better....that is when I runaway. I told them I needed to go home...but they wouldn't let me go...I told them, my daddy is dying. He is dead.

I felt I have no freedom; I have no peace. It feels like I am in prison. If you go outside, you are followed; even to take the trash out someone from the family follows you.

How did you find a way to leave?

In the apartment above, there are gates that those people used to go out. I don't know what happened that day because they are always locked. But not this day.

I ran to the American Embassy. But they told me they don't take in those issues and they directed me to the Ethiopian Embassy. They fetched me a cab and even paid for it. But I think the taxi driver did not know where that is....so we drove and drove...finally I say "ok, do you know the British Embassy?" and he took me there. I complained to them and they say I cannot stay, that they are closing, and that I have to go and come back the next day. I tell them I have nowhere to go. I tell them I cannot go back. But that place is big. There were these brick walls and I sat and slept the night between the walls. I was having my menses; I did not take a bath. I was scared.

But I went back in the morning and two people interviewed me and after the interview they said they cannot do anything about it. So I didn't know what to do about it either. I got another taxi and ask if he knew Ethiopian embassy and this one did. They kept me there for one day. The ambassador called a Nigerian pastor who knew of a Ghana organization. I could not stay at the Ethiopian embassy because I am not from that country. So the man and wife of the Ghana organization came. But said we cannot take you to our house because if police find you we also will be in trouble, so they said they were going to take me to the police station. Fortunately that pastor phoned to see how I was and they told her they were going to take me to the police station. Thankfully she intervened and said "let me do something first". I think that is when she called Aban (who belonged to her church). Immediately, Aban said to bring me over. That is how I got to the shelter.

You must have been terrified

oh I tell you...I tell you, I was...what a mess....I could trust............ nobody

Adjoua has now been in Kuwait 4 ½ years. Her young daughter, who turned ten this year, is living with her widowed mother.

Are you any closer to getting home?

This is not what I want. But my problem is...if I go back home now I will have no work. I have a daughter. My dad is gone and my mom is very weak so she cannot work. Right now if I do go home, it is with nothing. I haven't improved myself learning a trade in Kuwait as was promised, and I don't have courses, to add to myself. There is no money to do that....If I go home now with no job...who is going to take care of my mother and daughter and pay my daughters school fees...and all that .

So I stay working in Kuwait and send money home. I have no other choice. If I do, (go home) it makes it worse for them. My daughter can't go to school.

This is a big sacrifice you are doing for your family, Adjoua.

She is silent...a heavy sigh. "Yea". There's a long silence. Yea you are right. Because if I don't do it, tearfully she tells me, I have gone through a lot and still going through a lot. I don't know when all this trouble is going to end. But, my pastor says I am a strong person because you know, those girls I came here with? They have all gone back home...and I am still here. I have been here as a housemaid again for 7 months now. I haven't had my visa or passport for last 7 months. I *was working at a salon but I needed a visa 20, not 18 so I am not allowed to work, I had to leave. So I paid someone 600 KD (approximately $2100.00) to give me a two year visa and the person took my money and took my passport and I don't know where he is. Sobbing she says....He took my money ...he took my money and my passport away. So right now I can't go out. I don't go out. I am always in the house. I feel like I am in jail, ya know, and I don't know what to do. I don't like what I am doing right now, but I have no choice. I have to do it.*

We just sat together at our computer screens; neither one of us speaking. The effect of her sharing emotionally over-whelmed us both.

In the last month...they kick you out of country....even for a little mistake....even if you have visa. I am living in fear always.

If caught, she believes they would keep her in jail until they find the man who took her papers. *So I wonder how long they would keep me there. How long do I stay in this house? How long is this family staying in Kuwait? There is no Ghana embassy in Kuwait.....how will I to get my new papers? I need to find the man, or I cannot get a different job.*

I ask, do you write about it like in a journal?
No......but I will remember all that I am going through. I could make a film out of it, she says with a wry smile.
Lots of silence

I decided to lighten it a little and turn our focus on the shelter. I asked for her thoughts regarding the volunteers coming for an hour or two here and there.
It was a good thing...a sacrifice you were doing...the girls at the shelter were able to make things to sell...that was a good thing....and the girls have learned different skills. I was

given my own machine and I am doing sewing bit by bit. Last time someone saw me sewing the bed cover and they asked me where did you learn to sew...I said, here in Kuwait. Yeah, someone came to the shelter to teach me how to do this...and that is a good thing.

Sometimes you would come there and would talk to us you know. It made me feel we have people behind us. You know, people standing behind us....because sometimes lot of the girls go through a lot of pain...sewing gave us a focus....to give us a break from it....instead of thinking all the time...just to do something. That was a good thing you were doing. Let me tell you something, I remember one time that you came, I was very sad, and I was nearly crying and you hugged me...and I felt a little better. What I am trying to say is your presence in the shelter always made me feel better. Whenever you volunteers were working there, I felt so much better.

As of spring 2014 Adoua continues living in Kuwait unable to secure documents that would either give her freedom to work and live where she would like and/or give her the opportunity to return to Ghana. Her heart's desire is to become a nurse.

We continue to visit via Skype each week. My hope and prayer for her is that she will find freedom one day soon to pursue her dreams.

There is a new face of slavery.

There are more slaves in the world today than were taken from Africa in the four centuries of the Trans-Atlantic slave trade – over 27 million. We in the West have a hard time believing that this is really happening; that the forcible exploitation of humans for profit is not only alive and well in the 21ˢᵗ century but worse than ever before. - The Human Face of Modern Slavery

— Corban Addison

Human trafficking is the trade of humans, most commonly for the purpose of sexual slavery, forced labor, or commercial sexual exploitation for the trafficker or others. Human trafficking can occur within a country or trans-nationally. Human trafficking is a crime against the person because of the violation of the victim's rights of movement through coercion and because of their commercial exploitation.

Human trafficking represents an estimated $32 billion of international trade per annum, of the illegal international trade estimated at $650 billion per annum in 2010.

Human trafficking is condemned as a violation of human rights by international conventions definition. - Wikipedia

The United Nations defines human trafficking as *the recruitment, transportation, transfer, harboring or receipt of persons, by means of the threat or use of force or other forms of coercion, of abduction, fraud, of deception, of the abuse of power or a position of vulnerability or of the giving or receiving of payments or benefits to achieve the consent of a person having control over another person, for the purposes of exploitation.*

Trafficking is the term most frequently used to describe this phenomenon but slavery is a more accurate and descriptive term. Sex trafficking is the new face of slavery because it retains many of the same characteristics of a slave (trafficking victim)/master (trafficker) relationship. Women and girls are purchased cheaply and sold to customers at a high profit margin. Rather than serve one master or in one locale, victims are passed around among a variety of "owners. And because of the seemingly endless supply of women and girls, slaves are ultimately disposable. –Bales, Kevin Disposable People: New slavery in the Global Economy. University of California Press, 2004

Occasionally, women and girls are rescued from traffickers and receive support, care and compassion. More often, though, trafficking victims are treated like criminals by the police. Women and girls arrested in international trafficking circles are often processed as illegal immigrants rather than trafficking victims and are immediately deported to their home countries where, because few economic alternatives exist, they begin the cycle of trafficking and exploitation all over again.

I have personally witnessed only a glimpse of the injustice and brutality inflicted upon women and girls while living in Kuwait. The more I read, the more determined I become to spread the truth of this worldwide crime.

There are many organizations targeting a variety of ways to help end what has become a paramount human rights problem of the century.

Below I have listed just a few organizations, amongst many, that are accomplishing much to bring freedom, equality and education to women of all nations.

www.givewell.net Give Well is a nonprofit dedicated to finding outstanding giving opportunities and publishing the full details of our analysis to help donors decide where to give.

www.rrcaht.org   The Rochester Regional Coalition against Human Trafficking (RRCAHT) is dedicated to eliminating human trafficking in our communities through education, advocacy, and networking with individuals and organizations.

www.angelsofmercyny.org   Our mission and focus is to help women and girls achieve FREEDOM, DIGNITY and RESTORATION through our coordinated efforts and faith in God

www.globalgiving.org   Global Giving is a charity fundraising web site that gives social entrepreneurs and non-profits from anywhere in the world a chance to raise the money that they need to improve their communities

www.worldhope.org   World Hope International is a Christian relief and development organization working with vulnerable and exploited communities to alleviate poverty, suffering and injustice.

www.hrw.org   Human Rights Watch defends the rights of people worldwide.

thecnnfreedomproject.blogs.cnn.com   joining the fight to end modern-day slavery and shine a spotlight on the horrors of modern-day slavery, amplify the voices of the victims, highlight success stories and help unravel the complicated tangle of criminal enterprises trading in human life.

www.womenforwomen.org   connects women sponsors with needy women in conflict or post conflict countries

www.womenthrive.org   is an international advocacy group focused on the needs of women in poor countries

www.thp.org   focuses on empowerment of women and girls to end hunger

www.ijm.org   a Christian-based organization that fights sex trafficking

endslaverynow.org   We all have a role in ending slavery in our communities and around the world. At End Slavery Now, we help you find yours.

notforsalecampaign.org   We work with people and communities to build a world where no one is for sale.

www.freetheslaves.net   Our goal: to end slavery in our lifetime.

www.state.gov/j/tip/rls/tiprpt/2014   US State department Trafficking In Persons report (TIP)

www.TheA21Campaign.org   We prevent trafficking through awareness and education

www.unwomen.org   United Nations Entity for Gender Equality and the Empowerment of Women

slaveryfootprint.org   "How Many Slaves Work For You?"

www.care.org   serving individuals and families in the poorest communities in the world

www.sharedhope.org   fights sex trafficking around the worldo

www.humantrafficking.org   empowerment through knowledge

www.globalmamas.org   Global Mamas community is comprised of thousands of people from around the world working together with the mission of creating prosperity for African women and their families

www.maitinepal.org   its special focus has always been on preventing trafficking for forced prostitution, rescuing flesh trade victims and rehabilitating them.

I highly recommend the book, HALF THE SKY by Nicholas D. Kristof and Sheryl WuDunn. It is a magnificent read and an inspiration, encouraging through the stories shared, of what can be done to make a difference in our world.

The following is a list of resources I have gained much knowledge from and have quoted throughout this book.

Wikipedia

Migrant-rights.org

Arab Times Newspaper

Kuwait Times Newspaper

Change.org

Human Rights Report 2010

Sadu House website

United Nations website

Article The Human Face of Slavery by Corban Addison

My main goal has been to open wide the eyes of those within my circle of family and friends with the hope of a ripple effect; to encourage and inspire others to see, hear and act.

Funds raised will be donated to various charitable organizations that specially support women who are exploited in labor and sexual human trafficking around the globe.

Whatever you think you can do,

begin it.

Action has magic,

grace and power in it.

- Goethe